T0116604

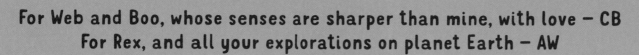

For Web and Boo, whose senses are sharper than mine, with love — CB
For Rex, and all your explorations on planet Earth — AW

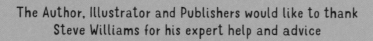

The Author, Illustrator and Publishers would like to thank
Steve Williams for his expert help and advice

Text copyright © Catherine Barr 2020
Illustrations copyright © Anne Wilson 2020
First published in Great Britain in 2020 by Otter-Barry Books,
Little Orchard, Burley Gate, Herefordshire, HR1 3QS
www.otterbarrybooks.com

All rights reserved

No part of this publication may be reproduced, stored in a retrieval system,
or transmitted, in any form, or by any means, electrical, mechanical, photocopying,
recording or otherwise without the prior written permission of the publisher
or a licence permitting restricted copying. In the United Kingdom
such licences are issued by the Copyright Licensing Agency, Barnard's Inn,
86 Fetter Lane, London EC4A 1EN
A catalogue record for this book is available from the British Library.

ISBN 978-1-910959-67-1

Illustrated with mixed media and digital

Printed in China
9 8 7 6 5 4 3 2 1

Invisible
Nature

A Secret World Beyond Our Senses

Written by **Catherine Barr**

Illustrated by **Anne Wilson**

Otter-Barry BOOKS

Invisible Nature
Invisible sights, silent sounds, odourless smells and mysterious forces

Have you ever wondered how dolphins find friends,
vampire bats zoom in on victims, why reindeer food glows in the snow,
or even how a duck-billed platypus finds its worm?

These animals and many others use light, scent, sound
and forces beyond our human senses to survive.
But though we cannot feel, see, smell or hear their secret world,
we use it every day in ways that might surprise you.

Get started with the Big Bang, go on to discover
how animals use mysterious natural powers and
find out how people have learned to use them too.

Contents

Follow me to
find out more!

Big Bangs and Silent Waves
The secret world of microwaves

Our universe began in a moment called the Big Bang. This gigantic fireball created light that has been spreading outwards through space ever since. Its light waves have stretched into microwaves as the universe expanded. We cannot see them, but by studying these cosmic microwaves scientists can work out how old our universe really is.

Explore microwaves in space.

Our universe is about 13.8 billion years old.

In 1964, two astronomers noticed a hazy hum coming from all directions of the universe. They thought it was caused by pigeon poo on their radio telescope, but found that this hum is caused by microwaves in space.

The afterglow of the Big Bang is a bit like a fog that fills the whole universe.

Scientists investigating cosmic microwaves fix their telescopes to satellites or put them on high mountains to get the best signal.

9

Microwaves... in our lives

On Earth, we have invented machines to make microwaves. We use them in medicine, in communications like phones, televisions and satellites and of course to heat food in microwave ovens.

Mobile phones and computers use microwaves... to send signals and messages.

Airports and ships use microwaves... to make 'radar' maps from microwave echoes bouncing back from objects in the sea and air.

WAVY FACTS

- Microwaves travel at the speed of light.

- Microwaves created by the Big Bang are called Cosmic Microwave Background Radiation (CMBR).

- Microwaves can pass straight through clouds, fog, rain and snow.

Space cameras use microwaves... to take clear pictures of Earth right through the clouds.

Doctors use microwave heat... to kill unwanted cells in our bodies that can cause illnesses like cancer. This is called Radiotherapy.

Cooks use microwaves... to heat food quickly in microwave ovens.

Day Glow and Shiny Colours
The secret world of ultraviolet

Ultraviolet (UV) light waves are powerful rays from the sun
that can damage many forms of life on Earth. Luckily a blanket
of gases shields our planet from most of the sun's UV radiation.
We cannot see UV light but some animals can, and they rely on it
for their survival.

Explore ultraviolet in the Canadian Arctic.

Lichens glow in UV, making it possible
for hungry reindeer to find this precious
food in barren Arctic habitats.

UV colour and patterns on plants help bees and butterflies
find nectar, helping pollination take place.

12

Butterflies use ultraviolet spots on their wings to send secret signals to one another and show off to attract mates.

Sockeye Salmon spot their prey, plankton, when it shows against UV light in shallow water.

Sweat, saliva and urine glow in UV, helping rats and other animals to trace their prey and survive in deep winter snow.

Ultraviolet... in our lives

We cannot see UV but from medicine to lighting, food and clothing, it plays an important role in our lives.

GLOWING FACTS

◎ 10% of sunlight is UV but only one third of this reaches Earth.

◎ Over-exposure to UV radiation can damage living things.

◎ Suncream protects our skin from harmful UV rays.

The food industry uses UV... to kill germs in water and food.

Our bodies use UV... to create valuable vitamin D when it shines on our skin, strengthening our bones and muscles.

Lights use UV... to shine with artificially created UV in fluorescent and other bulbs.

Cyclists use UV... to keep safe with high visibility clothing made of material that changes UV light into visible light, so it stands out.

Hot Waves and Night Shapes
The secret world of infrared

Infrared waves are invisible to humans and most other animals. Instead, many living things feel infrared as heat. Some animals have special infrared sensors that help them 'see' or 'feel' infrared heat, so they can find food and spot danger.

Discover infrared in forests and rivers in North and South America.

Some beetles are lured by the infrared of forest fires, where these 'fire bugs' lay their eggs in hot ash.

16

Vampire Bats use infrared to zoom in on their victims.

Blood-sucking mosquitos and bed bugs seek out their prey by feeling the 'heat' of waves of infrared.

Boa constrictors and rattlesnakes have a special infrared sensor in a pit between their eyes.

Piranhas and Goldfish use infrared to find food in murky waters.

17

Infrared... in our lives

We can use night goggles or special infrared cameras to create colourful pictures that reveal the secret and useful world of infrared.

You can use infrared... to make toast, or by pressing the TV remote to switch channels.

The police use infrared... to find people who are lost or hiding from them.

HOT FACTS

◎ Infrared waves are just beyond the colour red on our visible spectrum.

◎ We feel infrared waves as heat from sunlight or a fire.

◎ The hotter something is, the more infrared it radiates.

Space scientists use infrared... to spot stars in clouds of gas and dust.

Fast-food cafés use infrared... to keep food warm on the counter under infrared lamps.

Wildlife rangers use infrared... to seek and protect hibernating bears in dark caves.

Magnetic Powers and Electric Waves
The secret world of electromagnetism

Electromagnetism is one of the strongest forces in nature. Some animals use this invisible force to find food and work out where they are.

Discover electromagnetic secrets in Australian lands and seas.

The Duck-Billed Platypus is the only land mammal to have electric sensors – 40,000 in stripes along its bill that help it find worms and shrimps.

Solar winds make dark skies flash with amazing shows of light, the auroras, around the Earth's magnetic poles.

Migratory birds like the Curlew, famous for its record-breaking non-stop flight across the Pacific Ocean, may use a 'magnetic map' in their heads to find their way.

Honey Bees can detect tiny electric fields around flowers to work out if another bee has recently visited and perhaps taken all of the sugary prize.

Hammerhead Sharks hunt in murky waters using tiny, jelly-filled sensors on their heads. These pick up electromagnetic signals from the movement of their prey.

Electromagnetism... in our lives

We use electricity to power our modern lives but we also use the electromagnetic force every day in all sorts of surprising ways.

Compasses use magnets... to help us find our way by pointing North and South in the Earth's magnetic field.

N

W

E

S

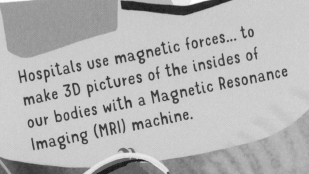

Hospitals use magnetic forces... to make 3D pictures of the insides of our bodies with a Magnetic Resonance Imaging (MRI) machine.

Electric doorbells and buzzers use magnets... to make familiar noises in our homes and schools.

ATTRACTIVE FACTS

- Microwaves, UV, infrared and visible light are all electromagnetic energy waves.

- The flow of electric currents is called electricity.

- The Earth's magnetic force is strongest at the North and South poles.

Loudspeakers and headphones use magnets... to power our music and play tunes out loud.

Magnet

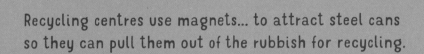

Recycling centres use magnets... to attract steel cans so they can pull them out of the rubbish for recycling.

Bouncing Sounds and Squeaky Whistles
The secret world of ultrasound

Some birds, bats, whales and dolphins communicate with special high-pitched sound waves called ultrasound. When ultrasound waves bump into something, they bounce back, making echoes. Animals use this 'echolocation' to help them find their way around and locate food.

Discover ultrasound in Europe and its seas.

Dolphins use complicated whistles and clicks to find food and keep track of one another in large travelling groups.

Bats bounce ultrasound around so they don't bump into things in the dark caves where they gather in their thousands.

The Greater Wax Moth has record-breaking ears... it can hear higher-pitched noises than any animal on Earth.

Hunting in the dark or in rough seas, Killer Whales and Sperm Whales use ultrasound to find shoals of fish and catch their prey.

Cats and dogs track mice and other small animals that make high-pitched squeaks to communicate with one another.

Ultrasound... in our lives

We cannot hear ultrasound, the high-pitched noises that travel through deep oceans, across dark caves and through open skies. But we use it every day in many different ways.

Dog owners use ultrasound... to train pets with special high-pitched whistles that only dogs can hear.

QUIET FACTS

- Ultrasound travels through solids, liquids or gas but not a vacuum, like space.

- When animals use ultrasound, it is called 'echolocation'.

- When people use ultrasound to measure distances and find objects underwater, it is called 'sonar'.

Hospitals use ultrasound... to take pictures of unborn babies and the insides of our bodies.

In some places ultrasound is used... to stop teenagers hanging about, by sending out annoying mosquito-like noises that only young people can hear. Many people disapprove of this.

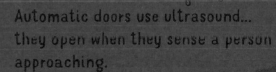

Automatic doors use ultrasound... they open when they sense a person approaching.

Submarines use ultrasound... to scan and map the ocean with sound bleeps and their echoes.

Shuddering Earth and Underwater Songs
The secret world of infrasound

Deep, low sounds travel a long way. This infrasound travels faster through land and sea than through the air. On underwater migrations and journeys on land, some animals use these deep sounds to communicate. They are keeping in touch and looking for mates in lonely oceans or in distant lands.

Discover infrasound in Asia's forests, rivers and oceans.

Elephants send vibrations through the ground with their feet to find other herds, warn of predators and seek mates in the wilderness.

Male alligators make vibrating infrasound across the water to attract females from far away.

Squid, Cuttlefish and Baleen Whales send mysterious deep sound waves through vast seas to communicate with others of their own kind.

Sumatran Rhinos make a song-like whistle followed by a sharp burst of air that can carry for up 20 kilometres (13 miles) through deep forest.

Tigers use low booming sounds that carry over long distances to scare rivals and attract mates.

Infrasound... in our lives

We cannot hear the rumble of an erupting volcano or the faraway stamp of an elephant's foot, but by using special microphones, people all over the world tap into the secrets of infrasound.

RUMBLING FACTS

◎ Infrasound travels around objects rather than through them.

◎ Low, deep sound sometimes makes humans feel chilly and uncomfortable.

◎ Researchers are exploring the impact of infrasound on people who spend time in noisy ships or on shuddering rockets.

Weather forecasters use infrasound... to listen out for approaching thunderstorms and high winds.

Doctors use infrasound... to study our hearts, which send infrasound vibrations around our bodies.

Space scientists use infrasound... to track the paths of meteors as they enter our atmosphere.

Conservationists use infrasound... to track migrations and protect animals on their long journeys.

Geologists use infrasound... to work out when volcanoes might erupt.

Weird Whiffs and Silent Smells
The world of secret scents

Beyond our human noses, there are clouds of scent, smelly trails and mysterious odours that animals use to communicate with one another, find prey, avoid predators, mark territory and find mates. From ants to sharks, all kinds of animals use smell to survive.

Discover secret scents in the Andes and Southern seas.

Dogs use an amazing sense of smell to explore their world. Their sense of smell is 1,000 to 10,000 times better than a human's.

Like all bears, Spectacled Bears depend on their noses to survive... in the cloud forests they smell ripe fruit or rotting meat many miles away.

The Albatross has an extraordinary sense of smell.
Big nostrils on this bird's beak help it sniff food
floating on water up to 20 kilometres (13 miles) away.

Sometimes known as 'swimming
noses', sharks can find prey by
smelling only a distant drop of
blood in the water.

Ants have the best sense of smell in the insect
world - it helps them communicate so they can
live together in a very organised way.

Secret scents... in our lives

We may be able to sniff a trillion smells. Scientists have realised that the human sense of smell is sharper than they thought, but we still make good use of animal super-smellers.

STINKY FACTS

◉ Women have a much better sense of smell than men.

◉ Most animals with a good sense of smell have poor vision.

◉ Some snakes flick their tongues to smell.

Medical teams in Tanzania and Mozambique use Giant African Pouched Rats... to smell cases of the killer disease tuberculosis.

Scientists use fruit flies... to smell human cancer cells, and help research this disease.

Armies use rats... to find and expose landmines so they can get rid of them forever.

Some airports use dogs and may even use Honey Bees... to sniff out problems at security check-ins.

Glossary

Cosmic: relates to everything in the universe except Earth.

Electric field: the area in which an electric charge works.

Electromagnetic radiation: energy waves that fill the universe. They include radio waves, microwaves, infrared waves, visible light, and ultraviolet waves: all are invisible to humans except visible light waves.

Light waves: the way that all kinds of light travel.

Magnetic field: the area in which a magnetic force works.

Radar: the use of radio waves to find the position or movement of an object.

Sound waves: the way that sound travels, by vibrations through solids, liquids and gases.

Visible spectrum: the range of light waves that humans can see.

Invisible Nature and You

Sound waves
(dogs hear more)

Earth scents
(trillions of them)

Visible spectrum
(all the light waves we can see)

Infrared rays
(feel the warmth)

Ultraviolet rays
(ouch, sunburn)

Cosmic microwaves and Radio waves
(didn't feel a thing)

Earth's electromagnetism
(protecting us from harmful cosmic rays)

SUN

UNIVERSE